IN THE STEPS OF THE
APOSTLE PAUL

F. F. Bruce

KREGEL
PUBLICATIONS

Grand Rapids, MI 49501

The Forum,
Rome.

'I am not ashamed of the gospel, because it is the power of God for the salvation of everyone who believes.' (Romans 1:16)

IN THE STEPS OF
THE APOSTLE PAUL

F. F. BRUCE

PHOTOGRAPHS BY MAURICE S. THOMPSON

Paul's Missionary Journeys

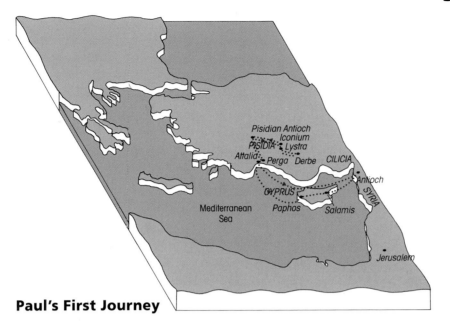

Paul's First Journey

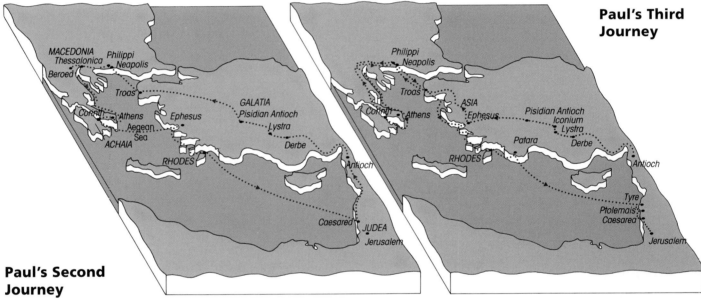

Paul's Second Journey

Paul's Third Journey

Paul's Journey to Rome

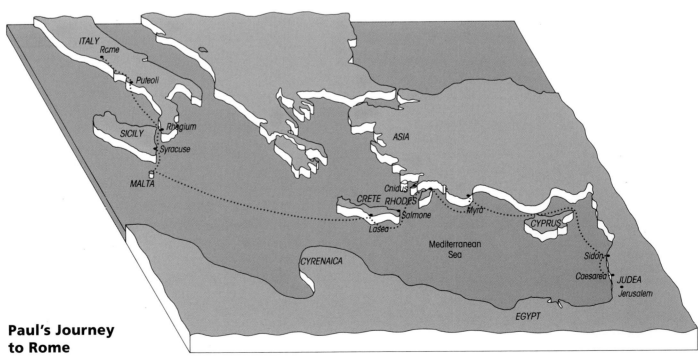

Contents

Paul's Life

AD 5	Born in Tarsus
35	Converted on the road to Damascus
35-38	Ministers in Arabia and Damascus (*Galatians 1:17*)
38	Visits Jerusalem (*Galatians 1:18*)
38-43	Ministers in Syria and Tarsus (*Galatians 1:21*)
43-46	Serves in Antioch with Barnabas
47-49	First Missionary Journey (*Acts 13-14*)
49	Apostles' Council in Jerusalem (*Acts 15*)
50	Writes Letter to Galatians
50-52	Second Missionary Journey (*Acts 15:36-18:22*)
52-55	Third Missionary Journey (*Acts 18:23-21:16*)
55-58	Writes Letter to Romans
56	Journey to Jerusalem: Arrested (*Acts 21*)
57-59	Imprisoned in Caesarea
59	Journey to Rome (*Acts 27*)
60-61	Imprisoned in Rome
61	Released from prison
61-65	Ministers in Asia Minor and Greece
65	Arrested, tried and executed in Rome

All dates are approximate.

Left: The ancient agora, Athens.

Introduction

Within a few years of Jesus' resurrection, the young church in Jerusalem, led by Peter and the apostles, was being persecuted by the Jewish religious leaders. Stephen's death, witnessed by a young Pharisee named Saul, is recorded by Luke in the Acts of the Apostles. This is the first time we meet the man who was to evangelise the Roman Empire.

Paul's conversion on the way to Damascus happened within a few years of Pentecost. After his encounter with the risen Christ, Paul visited Damascus briefly, spent some time in Arabia, modern Jordan, and visited Jerusalem two or three years later. He embarked at Caesarea for the sea-crossing to Tarsus, where he stayed for about ten years, preaching the gospel.

Paul started preaching and teaching in Tarsus not more than five years after Jesus'

ascension. Within fifteen years he had gone to help Barnabas in Antioch, and from there Paul and Barnabas began their travels to Cyprus and Asia Minor. The gospel reached Macedonia within twenty years of the ascension, and Paul was in Greece by about AD 50. On his return to Jerusalem, Paul was taken by the Roman army to Caesarea, where he was imprisoned AD 57-9. His trial was transferred to Rome, which he reached early in AD 60, and where he stayed under house arrest. His death was probably in Nero's persecution of the Christians in AD 64 or shortly afterwards.

Paul's story begins in Tarsus, where he was born; but we first meet him in Jerusalem, which had not changed greatly since the years Jesus visited it.

We take up Paul's story again in Damascus, and follow his travels through present-day Syria, Turkey, Greece and Italy.

Above: A water-carrier in modern Tarsus, Paul's birthplace.

Right: The Damascus Gate, Jerusalem, still today a busy entrance to the Old City.

Tarsus

'I am a Jew,' said Paul to the officer commanding the Roman garrison in the Antonia fortress in Jerusalem, 'from Tarsus in Cilicia, a citizen of no mean city' (Acts 21: 39).

Tarsus, Paul's birthplace, was the principal city of Cilicia, the most south-easterly part of Asia Minor. It stood in a fertile plain, on both banks of the river Cydnus, about ten miles from its mouth. The river was navigable as far upstream as Tarsus. Some thirty miles north of Tarsus were the Cilician Gates – the pass through the Taurus range which carried the main road from Syria into central Asia Minor. It is still a well-populated city, with about 40,000 inhabitants.

Tarsus was a city of great antiquity: it was a fortified trading centre before 2000 BC and is mentioned in Hittite records of the second millennium BC. It was destroyed in the invasions of the sea-peoples about 1200 BC, but some time later it was refounded by Greek settlers. For short periods in the ninth and seventh centuries BC it fell under Assyrian control. It enjoyed considerable autonomy under the Persian Empire, as capital of the satrapy of Cilicia; it was even permitted to issue its own coinage. In due course it passed into the hands of Alexander the Great. After his death in 323 BC it belonged to the dynasty of Seleucus I and his descendants, who succeeded to the eastern part of Alexander's empire. Under this dynasty it was called Antioch-on-Cydnus, but the name did not stick.

When Pompey established Roman dominance in that part of the world (67 BC), Tarsus became part of the Roman Empire, but retained its privileges as a free city. It was capital of the Roman province of Cilicia until 25 BC,

but in that year Eastern Cilicia (in which Tarsus was situated) was detached from Western Cilicia and united with the province of Syria. It was Tarsus that witnessed the romantic first meeting of Antony and Cleopatra, described by Plutarch and embellished by Shakespeare.

In the later part of Antony's control of the Near East, Tarsus suffered under the maladministration of a nominee of his named Boethus. When Augustus overthrew Antony and became sole master of the Roman world, he entrusted the administration of Tarsus to one of its most illustrious sons, Athenodorus the Stoic, who had been Augustus's own tutor. Athenodorus

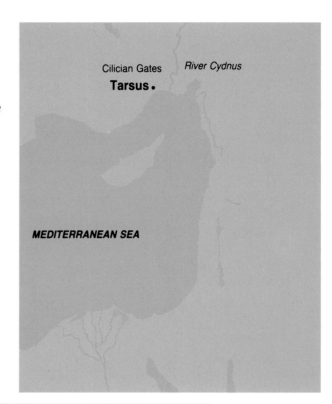

Cilician Gates · River Cydnus
Tarsus.

MEDITERRANEAN SEA

Left: The Apostle Paul as depicted in a twelfth- or thirteenth-century mosaic at Monreale Cathedral, Sicily. Paul is by tradition shown as a short, bald-headed man.

'... a citizen of no mean city ... ' (Acts 21:39)

reformed the city's constitution; it was probably he who fixed a property qualification of 500 drachmae for admission to the burgess roll too.

Tarsus was a well-known centre of culture. Its schools taught the whole round of learning – philosophy and the liberal arts. In modern terms we might speak of the University of Tarsus though it was a civic university catering for Tarsians, whereas both Athens and Alexandria attracted many students from distant lands.

It was a prosperous city, renowned for some of its material products. Several authors refer to the linen which was manufactured there from the flax which grew in the fertile plain around the city. We also hear of a cloth called *cilicium*, woven from goat's hair, which gave welcome protection against cold and wet. It may have been from this cloth that Paul learned to make tents. Perhaps he came of a tent-making family. His family appears to have been well-to-do, and over and above its economic prosperity it had received the rare honour of Roman citizenship. When Paul claimed to have been born a Roman citizen, this implied that his father had been a Roman citizen before him (Acts 22:28). How Roman citizenship came into the family we do not know. One archaeological scholar suggested that a firm of tent-makers could have proved very useful to the Roman army in those parts and received the citizenship as a reward 'for services rendered'.

Although Paul was born in Tarsus, he may not have spent long there as a child. We may gather from Acts 22:3 that he grew up in Jerusalem. His parents were devout Jews, and probably judged that Jerusalem would be a more suitable environment for their son in his formative years than the pagan city of Tarsus.

At a later date, however, after his conversion, Paul spent some years in and around Tarsus. After he had paid a short visit to Jerusalem in the third year after his conversion he was taken from there to Caesarea by some friends and put on board a ship bound for Tarsus (Acts 9:30). There, perhaps nine or ten years later, Barnabas found him and persuaded him to join him in Antioch and share the oversight of the Christian mission there (Acts 11:25, 26). We have no details of the years that Paul spent in and around Tarsus, but he was actively engaged in his apostolic ministry. It was during those years that

Left: The Cilician Gates, the pass through the Taurus Mountains carrying the main route from Syria into central Asia Minor. The pass lies about 30 miles north of Tarsus.

Above: A diptych such as this could have contained a certificate of Paul's birth registration, establishing his claim to Roman citizenship.

news kept coming to the churches in Judea: 'Our former persecutor is now preaching the faith which he once tried to destroy' (Galatians 1:23).

Considerable excavation has been carried out in the Tarsus area, mainly on the mound called Gözlü Kule, where there was a western outpost of the Hellenistic and Roman city. (The adjective 'Hellenistic' refers to the Greek period from the conquests of Alexander the Great onwards.) The city's Roman theatre has been uncovered on Gözlü Kule, but the main buildings of the Roman period lie buried beneath modern Tarsus. Many buildings of Roman Tarsus are mentioned by contemporary writers, but

A Man of Tarsus

On the first occasion when Tarsus is mentioned in the New Testament, it is one of the indications given to Ananias of Damascus, who is being sent to speak to Paul, to help in identifying him. Ananias is told to go to such-and-such a street and knock at the door of a certain person's house, and ask for 'a man of Tarsus named Saul; for behold, he is praying' (Acts 9:11). Paul was part of the apostle's name as a Roman citizen, but as he was born into an observant Jewish family, belonging to the tribe of Benjamin (Romans 11:1; Philippians 3:5), his parents gave him a Jewish name – the name of the most illustrious member of the tribe of Benjamin in the history of Israel, King Saul. This was the name by which he was known in Jewish circles. Ananias would recognise him by three distinguishing features. The first two – his name and the name of his birthplace – are those which we should expect to be mentioned. The third – 'he is praying' – makes one think.

only a few survive, and that in fragmentary form. These include the immense foundations of a temple, and a building decorated with mosaics which was discovered when foundations were being dug for a new courthouse in 1947. On the occasions when reconstruction is undertaken in the modern city, it is usually Byzantine remains that come to light.

Damascus

Damascus was a very ancient city by the time Paul journeyed there to arrest Christian refugees from Jerusalem. It occupied the same site as the Damascus of Old Testament times, but had changed beyond recognition. Since the eighth century BC it had been dominated in turn by the Assyrians, Babylonians and Persians, and then by Alexander the Great. After Alexander's death (323 BC) it was controlled first by the dynasty of the Ptolemies in Egypt and then (after 200 BC) by the rival dynasty of the Seleucids, whose capital city was Antioch.

When the Seleucid power collapsed, Damascus fell for a few years under the control of the kingdom of the Nabataean Arabs, which stretched from the vicinity of Damascus south to the Gulf of Aqaba, with its capital at Petra. But with the arrival of the Romans under Pompey in 64 BC, Damascus learned to live with a new and more durable master. It was included in the Roman province of Syria, but was linked in a loose federation with a number of cities farther south – the Decapolis or 'league of ten cities'.

Not much of Roman Damascus is to be seen now. The east gate (*Bab esh-Sharqi*) may be of Roman date; it originally had three arches, but two of them have been walled up. In Hellenistic times Damascus was completely re-planned on the Hippodamian grid-system (so called after Hippodamus of Miletus, a town-planner of the fifth century BC). It had all the public installations which were regarded as essential to a Hellenistic city. When Herod the Great presented it with a gymnasium and a theatre, these were presumably designed to supersede earlier ones.

In Roman times Greek was the language most commonly

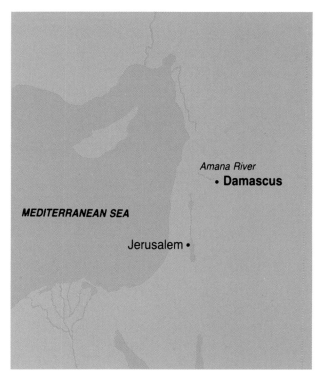

heard in Damascus, but Aramaic would have been spoken there too, as it had been in the days of Ben-hadad and other Aramaean kings of whom we read in the Old Testament. Aramaic was

Below: A view over the modern city of Damascus from the mountains to the west of the city.

Left: The 'Street called Straight', Damascus, Paul's first refuge when blinded on the road. Here he was visited by Ananias.

Right: The river Barada enters the oasis of Damascus. This is the river known as 'Abana' in 2 Kings 5:12.

the language of the Nabataean Arabs, who had a colony in Damascus administered by an ethnarch (mentioned in 2 Corinthians 11:32), and it would have been spoken by some members of the large Jewish community in the city.

Damascus figures in Muslim traditional belief as the place to which Jesus will descend at his second advent to destroy Antichrist (compare 2 Thessalonians 2:8). This belief may well go back beyond the Muslim conquest (AD 635), although it is not precisely documented before that.

In pre-Christian times there appears to have been a branch of the Qumran community in Damascus. This is inferred from a work called *The Book of the Covenant* of *Damascus*, discovered at the end of the nineteenth century in two incomplete manuscripts from the ancient synagogue of Old Cairo. This work tells of a body of pious Jews who 'went out from the land of Judah and sojourned in the land of Damascus', where they entered into a 'new covenant'. Not until the Qumran texts (the so-called Dead Sea Scrolls) came to

'In Damascus he had preached fearlessly ... '
(Acts 9:27)

Right: An elderly
man walks
through an alley
in the old
quarter of
Damascus.

light in 1947 and the following years was it realised that this body of pious Jews must have been associated with the Qumran community (the people of the Scrolls). It is not agreed by all that the 'Damascus' where they entered into a new covenant is to be understood literally and not figuratively, but most probably it is the literal Damascus that is meant. Those who made a covenant there believed that they were fulfilling Amos 5:27, which speaks of Jews going into exile beyond Damascus. These people's exile was largely voluntary, because they disapproved so utterly of the regime which at that time held power in Judea. They had a clear idea in their own minds of how events would unfold at the

time of the end, and one may wonder if they were the originators of the belief that Antichrist would meet his doom at Damascus.

One may wonder, too, if Paul had any contact with these 'covenanters' in Damascus after his conversion. His conversion took place as he was approaching Damascus with letters of extradition from the high priest in Jerusalem, authorising him to arrest and bring back in chains to Jerusalem followers of Jesus who had escaped from Jerusalem during the persecution that broke out after the stoning of Stephen. In one revolutionary flash he was confronted by the risen Christ. Against all his prejudice, he had no option now but to acknowledge the

Right: A narrow, arched street in the Old City quarter of Damascus.

'Saul spent several days with the disciples in Damascus.' (Acts 9:19)

Right The Chapel of Ananias, Damascus.

Far right: Columns and arches of the Roman temple of Jupiter in the Al-Hamidiyeh Souk, Damascus.

crucified Jesus as the risen Lord, who was there and then calling him into his service. The law of Israel, which had hitherto occupied the central place in Paul's life, was instantaneously displaced by Christ. From that moment on, for him 'to live was Christ' (Philippians 1:21).

Temporarily blinded by 'the glory of that light' which he had seen (Acts 22:11), Paul had to be led by the hand into Damascus, and there he lodged for some days in the house of a man named Judas, in the 'street called Straight' (Acts 9:11). The present *Darb al-Mustaqim* ('Straight Street'), otherwise known as *Suq et-Tawileh* ('Long Bazaar'), probably follows the line of that ancient street.

There he was visited by Ananias, a Jewish resident of Damascus, 'a devout man according to the law' (Acts 22:12), who confessed Jesus as Lord. Ananias greeted Paul as a brother and welcomed him into the company of Christ's followers. Ananias seems not to have been one of the refugees from Jerusalem whom Paul had been sent to apprehend, although he knew all about the purpose of Paul's visit. There were apparently two groups of disciples of Jesus in Damascus – members of the Jewish community there and others who had fled from the persecution in Judea. These were the people with whom Paul first found Christian fellowship. It would be interesting to know if Ananias, or some of his fellow-disciples, had any connection with the 'covenanters of Damascus'; but we have no means of knowing.

Paul did not stay long in Damascus. He visited those synagogues to which he had been accredited as the high priest's ambassador, but he visited them now as the ambassador of another master. In those synagogues he proclaimed Jesus, saying, 'He is the Son of God' (Acts 9:20). But the risen Christ had called him specifically to be his messenger to the Gentiles (Galatians 1:16), so he left Damascus and spent some time among the Nabataean Arabs (Galatians 1:17). His activity among them was sufficiently provocative to attract the hostile attention of the Nabataean king, Aretas IV (9 BC–AD 40), for on his return to Damascus the local representative of Aretas guarded the city gate in the hope of arresting him. Paul was forced to make his escape in a basket let down through a window in the city

Right: Damascus, Syria from the nearby hills.

wall (2 Corinthians 11:32, 33). It is believed by some historians that at this time Damascus formed part of the Nabataean kingdom, and it is pointed out that no Roman coins have been found at Damascus for the period AD 37–62. But this is by no means certain. Paul's escape from Damascus, at any rate, is the last occasion on which Damascus figures in the New Testament record.

The Sublime and the Ridiculous

There were two outstanding experiences associated with Damascus which Paul never forgot. One was unspeakably glorious: it was the revelation of Jesus Christ which he received or, as he puts it elsewhere, the occasion when he saw 'the light of the knowledge of the glory of God in the face of Christ' (2 Corinthians 4:6). The other was quite ridiculous: it was being let down in a basket through a window in the city wall to escape his enemies. But both taught him humility – the latter because, in his mind's eye, he must have cut such an absurd figure; the former because it brought home to him his total unworthiness to be granted such a revelation and to be called to serve the one who was revealed to him.

Jerusalem

Right: A Jewish boy carries the scroll of the Law at his barmitzvah at the Western Wall, Jerusalem.

Jerusalem as Paul knew it was small in scope but impressive in appearance. Its status as a holy city had been confirmed to it by successive Gentile overlords – Persian, Greek and Roman. In Jewish belief, Jerusalem was the city which the God of Israel had chosen 'to put his name and make his habitation there' (Deuteronomy 12:5). By Paul's day it had changed almost beyond recognition from the city that was hurriedly rebuilt by the impoverished Jews who returned from the Babylonian exile in 539 BC and the following years.

The main quarters of the city, however, remained much as they had been before: they were determined largely by natural features. The city was divided into two parts by the north–south line of the Tyropoeon Valley (the Valley of the Cheesemakers). East of that valley stood the Temple and associated buildings; south of the Temple stood the lower city, the eastern

Below: Jerusalem viewed from the Haas Promenade.

15

Above: Part of the Old City of Jerusalem viewed from the ramparts of the Damascus Gate.

Right: The Damascus Gate has been splendidly restored in recent times, and is often thronged with visitors.

section of which (Ophel) was the original Jerusalem which David captured from the Jebusites and chose as his own capital (2 Samuel 5:6-9). West of the Tyropoeon Valley was the upper city, which does not appear to have been settled so early as the lower city. The south-west quarter was evidently first occupied during the Judean monarchy.

Perhaps eighty years after the return from exile, an abortive attempt was made to surround the city with a wall (Ezra 4:12). The building of a wall was actually carried through by Nehemiah, in accordance with the decree of Artaxerxes I, king of Persia (445 BC). Nehemiah's wall probably enclosed the lower city and the south-western quarter. The Temple was separately enclosed. On the north, the wall probably followed the west–east line of the present King David Street running north of the south-western quarter and crossing the Tyropoeon Valley to meet the western wall of the Temple.

The walls of Jerusalem were repaired by the high priest Simon II about 200 BC

Opposite: The Church of the Holy Sepulchre, Jerusalem, built over the traditional site of Jesus' burial.

but they were broken down in 167 BC by Antiochus Epiphanes, who built a strong citadel in the city of David, south of the Temple. The city was refortified by the Hasmonaeans, and especially by John Hyrcanus (1 Maccabees 16:23).

Jerusalem was greatly beautified by Herod the Great, who erected or restored many fine buildings. Apart from the Temple, the most magnificent of all his

buildings, he rebuilt the fortress of Baris, north-west of the Temple area, and renamed it Antonia, after his patron Mark Antony; he built a palace for himself on the west wall of the city ('Herod's praetorium' of Acts 23:35) and three strong towers in its neighbourhood, one of which is incorporated in the present Citadel. He also built such public installations as an amphitheatre and a hippodrome.

16

Right: Remains of steps to Herod's Temple, Jerusalem, a building which would have been well known to the Apostle Paul.

Right: St. Stephen's Gate, Jerusalem. By tradition, it was outside this gate that Stephen, the first Christian martyr, was stoned to death. Paul was a witness of his death.

It was under Herod, if not earlier, that a second north wall was built to enclose the north-western quarter of the city: it began at an unidentified point called the Gate Gennath and ran in a northerly and then easterly direction, passing south of the present Church of the Holy Sepulchre, until it reached the Antonia fortress. The area of the walled city that Paul knew was about half a square mile (320 acres); its population may have been as high as 50,000. But already people were beginning to build dwelling-houses beyond the second north wall, in the section called Bezetha, or Newtown.

Antioch

There were sixteen cities called Antioch in the eastern Mediterranean world founded in the period after the death of Alexander the Great (323 BC). They owed their existence to rulers of the Seleucid dynasty which succeeded to the eastern part of Alexander's empire; many of the kings of that dynasty bore the name Antiochus, from which the place-name Antioch (*Antiocheia* in Greek) is derived. The greatest and best known of these cities is Antioch in North Syria, Antioch-on-the-Orontes, founded by Seleucus I, first king of the Seleucid dynasty, in 300 BC and called after his father Antiochus. The city and the name survive to this day in Antakya, in the Hatay province of Turkey, which has a population of about 40,000.

Antioch, being a new city, was constructed on the most up-to-date town-planning principles, according to the Hippodamian grid-system. It was built about sixteen miles upstream from the mouth of the river Orontes. At the mouth of the river stood its port, Seleucia Pieria (mentioned in Acts 13:4). The city walls of Antioch, the remains of which are still to be seen, ran along the hills overlooking the city and were extended seawards so as to enclose the port. (Similarly, the long walls of Athens in the fifth century BC were designed to protect the port of Piraeus and the approach to it.) Antioch originally stood on the south bank of the Orontes, but later kings extended it in various

Below: A view over the modern city of Antakya, ancient Antioch. In Paul's day it was the third largest city in the Roman Empire.

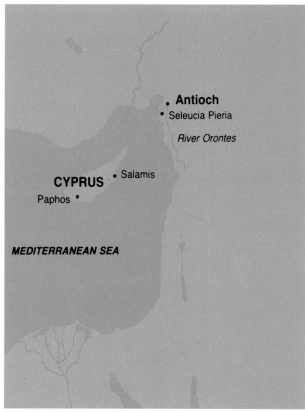

'The disciples were first called Christians at Antioch ... ' (Acts 11:26)

Above: A cobbled street typical of the older quarters of Antakya (ancient Antioch).

legate, who from 25 BC had charge of the united province of Syria and Cilicia. The city continued to be embellished with fine buildings: Herod the Great, for example, repaved its main east–west street with polished stone and adorned it with colonnades on both sides. The remains of this street and of another one, also colonnaded, can still be recognised. So can the remains of the circus (north of the Orontes), palace (on the Orontes island), colonnaded forum, theatre, amphitheatre and public baths. An impressive wealth of mosaics from the floors of these and other buildings has come to light. In New Testament times Antioch ranked as the third largest city of the Roman Empire; it was surpassed only by Rome and Alexandria.

Antioch features in the New Testament as the first headquarters of Gentile Christianity. Even before Christianity reached the city, one Nicolaus, called 'a proselyte of Antioch', was one of the seven men appointed in the church of Jerusalem to supervise the daily distribution from the common fund (Acts 6:5). From its earliest days, there was a very large Jewish community in Antioch, and Nicolaus presumably belonged to it, though it would hardly have been in his native city that he became a Christian at that early date. But only a few years later it was at Antioch that the gospel was first presented to Gentiles on any significant scale.

As a result of the persecution of the church in Judea that was launched immediately after the death of Stephen, some Hellenistic disciples (i.e. those whose first language was Greek and who had affinities with the provinces north-west and south-west of Palestine) made their way north through Syria till they came

directions. One of them built a new ward of the city on an island in the river; in this island the royal palace was situated. Another king extended the city southwards to the foot of Mount Silpius, which runs parallel with the river. As a result of these extensions the city came to comprise four wards; each of these was separately fortified apart from the fortifications surrounding the whole city.

Antioch had a plentiful supply of better drinking water than the Orontes could supply, from the fresh springs at Daphne, five miles to the

south. Here was a shrine dedicated to Artemis and Apollo. These were scarcely the Greek deities of those names; they were the Syrian goddess Astarte and her consort, newly equipped with Greek names. 'Daphnic morals' were a by-word in the Roman world for loose living. Antioch itself was sometimes distinguished from other cities of the same name by being called 'Antioch near Daphne'.

When Syria became a Roman province in 64 BC, Antioch became the seat of government of the imperial

Above: One of the many pools at Daphne, where in the Apostle's time there was an important shrine to Artemis and Apollo.

Right: The footpath on Mount Silpius leading to St. Paul's Cave, the refuge of persecuted Christians particularly during the time of the Emperor Diocletian.

to Antioch. Here some enterprising spirits among them – unnamed Jewish Christians from Cyprus and Cyrene – began to speak about Christ and his salvation to Gentiles whom they met. This was an innovation, but people were accustomed to innovations in Antioch. Here all sorts of nationality and religion met; here the Mediterranean world met the Syrian desert. People had their rough corners rubbed smooth, and traditional attitudes which were taken so seriously in a place like Jerusalem did not matter so much. Many Gentiles in Antioch, hearing the gospel for the first time, greeted it as the very message they were waiting for, and soon there was a flourishing church in Antioch, consisting mainly of Gentile believers. It was at Antioch that the followers of Jesus first came to be known as Christians; the name of Christ was so continually on their lips that they were recognised as his people.

When news of the innovation at Antioch came to the leaders of the mother-church in Jerusalem they did not panic but sent a suitable delegate to Antioch to see what was happening there

'Set apart for me Barnabas and Saul ... '
(Acts 13:2)

and give such guidance as he thought fit. The man they chose was Barnabas, a Jewish Christian from Cyprus and a foundation member of the Jerusalem church. Barnabas was not the name his parents had given him; he received it from his fellow-Christians because it expressed his encouraging character (it means 'the son of encouragement'). Barnabas came to Antioch and was delighted by what he found there. He settled down among the Christians of the place and gave them all the encouragement they needed as they prosecuted their forward movement of evangelism among the Gentiles of the city.

The work developed and the church increased at such a pace in Antioch that Barnabas soon felt unable to cope with it single-handed, so he fetched his friend Paul from Tarsus to come to Antioch and share his ministry. Under their joint guidance the Christian cause in the city continued to flourish. Gentiles though the majority of the Christians of Antioch were, they did not forget their link with the mother-church. When they learned of an impending famine that was likely to hit Jerusalem with special severity, they sent Barnabas and Paul there with a gift which they had collected to enable their brothers and sisters to face the steep rise in the cost of food.

The Christians of Antioch recognised that the gospel, which had met the need of so many people in their own city, was bound to meet the need of other Gentiles farther afield. On one occasion, when the will of God was made known through a prophetic utterance in their church, they readily released Barnabas and Paul to undertake an extended campaign of evangelism in Cyprus and Asia Minor.

The Christian mission to Gentiles was attended by some practical problems. It took some time before Jewish Christians, with their ancestral food restrictions and other social customs, learned to mix freely with Gentile Christians. There was one awkward occasion when Peter, on a visit to Antioch, felt obliged to desist from sharing meals with Gentile Christians because a message came to him telling of the embarrassment which his free-and-easy ways were causing to his fellow-disciples back home in Jerusalem. Not

long after this the church of Antioch sent a delegation to Jerusalem to have these matters discussed and settled at the highest level. The result was a social accommodation (Acts 15:28, 29) which continued to be observed by Gentile Christians for a long time. As late as the closing part of the ninth century Alfred the Great incorporated it in his English lawcode.

Antioch continued to be an important Christian centre for many centuries.

The 'Chalice of Antioch' is a silver cup set in a gilded

Above: The river Orontes as it flows from the city of Antioch towards the Mediterranean Sea.

Left: Inside the Crusader church which now encloses St. Paul's Cave on Mount Silpius.

Left: The rich green countryside betwen Antioch (modern Antakya) and Seleucia Pieria.

Above: The quiet waters of Paphos harbour, Cyprus, today. During Paul's visit the Roman proconsul, Sergius Paulus, was converted.

Above right: Assos, the seaport to which Paul walked from Troas (Acts 20:13,14).

open-work shell and mounted on a silver base, found in or near Antioch about 1910. It is now in the Metropolitan Museum of Art, New York. Some people liked to think at one time that the silver cup was the holy grail, the chalice used at the Last Supper; however its workmanship belongs to the fourth century AD.

The Birthplace of Gentile Christianity

Christianity has for many centuries been reckoned to be a Gentile religion. Yet it originated as a movement within the Jewish nation. The Founder of Christianity and all his apostles were practising Jews. If we ask how it became detached from its Jewish matrix and acquired its predominantly non-Jewish character, we

have to look to Antioch, the real birthplace of Gentile Christianity. The unnamed men of Cyprus and Cyrene who first thought of communicating the gospel to Gentiles in Antioch started something, the outcome of which they could never have foreseen.

Galatia

Galatia was a great Roman province in the heart of Asia Minor. It took its name from the Galatians, originally a group of Celts or Gauls that parted company with the main body of their fellow-tribesmen in Europe and moved south-east through the Balkan Peninsula, crossing into Asia Minor in the third century BC. There they settled in territory that had formerly belonged to the Phrygians. One of their principal cities, Ancyra, survives to the present day as the capital of Turkey, still bearing essentially the same name, Ankara.

The kings of Galatia became allies of the Romans, but when in 25 BC the last of those kings fell in battle against raiders from the Taurus mountain range, the Emperor Augustus took over his kingdom as a Roman province and incorporated in it a good deal of territory to the south, which the Galatian kings had never ruled.

We do not know if Paul ever visited that northern part of the province which had been the kingdom of Galatia. We do know of several cities in the southern part of the province which he visited. On the missionary tour, based in Antioch in Syria, which he undertook with Barnabas (Acts 13:4-14:26), he and Barnabas sailed from Paphos, the western capital of Cyprus, to

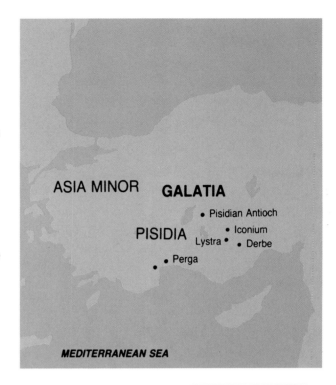

ASIA MINOR **GALATIA**

• Pisidian Antioch

PISIDIA   Lystra • • Iconium
                        • Derbe

• Perga

MEDITERRANEAN SEA

Below: The harbour at Antalya (ancient Attalia), the port from which Paul sailed back to Antioch at the end of his first missionary journey.

24

'Paul and his companions sailed to Perga ... '
(Acts 13:13)

Left: Colourful fishing boats moored in the harbour at Antalya, ancient Attalia, the port for Perga.

Right: Remains of the Roman amphitheatre at Perga, visited by Paul on his first missionary journey.

the south coast of Asia Minor, and made their way to Perga, an important city of the Roman province of Pamphylia, lying six miles inland. From there they struck up country until they reached Pisidian Antioch. After preaching there they moved on in succession to Iconium, Lystra and Derbe; then they retraced their steps through the same cities, turning south again from Pisidian Antioch until they reached the port of Attalia from which they sailed back to the mouth of the Orontes and so returned to the city of Antioch in Syria.

Two or three years later (perhaps in AD 49) Paul and Silas travelled from Antioch in Syria by land through the Cilician Gates into Central Asia Minor and visited Derbe and Lystra. From there they went on through 'the region of Phrygia and Galatia' (Acts 16:6) – that is, most probably, the region in which Iconium

'From Perga they went on to Pisidian Antioch... '
(Acts 13:14)

Right: View from the slopes of the plateau on which Pisidian Antioch stood. The site lies across the valley from the small Turkish town of Yalvaç. In the distance can be seen the remains of the ancient Roman aqueduct.

Right: Arches from the Roman aqueduct are prominent evidence for the ancient town of Pisidian Antioch, visited by Paul during his first missionary journey.

and Pisidian Antioch were situated. Just three years later Paul made a hasty journey through the same area when, making his way west to Ephesus, he is said to have passed through 'the region of Galatia and Phrygia' (Acts 18:23).

There is good reason to believe that 'the churches of Galatia' addressed in Galatians 1:2 were the churches planted by Paul and Barnabas in Pisidian Antioch, Iconium, Lystra and Derbe.

Pisidian Antioch stood on a plateau about 3,600 feet high, two miles west of the modern Turkish town of Yalvaç. Sir William Ramsay suggested that Paul caught malaria in the low-lying area around Perga and came to this high ground to recuperate: he thought that malaria might be the 'bodily ailment' from which, as Paul says in Galatians 4:13, he was

suffering when first he came to Galatia. This can be neither proved nor disproved.

Pisidian Antioch was founded as a border fortress soon after 300 BC. Augustus appreciated its strategic importance and made it a Roman colony in 6 BC. It became the military centre for the surrounding territory, and it was the starting-point for two roads built deep into the region of Pisidia to the south. Therefore, although it was not actually in Pisidia, it was known as Antioch near Pisidia, or Pisidian Antioch.

The site is now ruined, but the remains are still impressive. An aqueduct is particularly conspicuous; the city walls are also plainly to be seen. The main city square, the Square of Augustus, has been excavated; a monumental staircase and an entrance gateway (the propylaea) with three arches, connected it with the lower

Above: Lake Beysehir, eighty kilometres (fifty miles) west of Konya (ancient Iconium). It was through country such as this that the Apostle Paul and his companions travelled during their epic mission.

Left: The site of Pisidian Antioch, the hill on the opposite side of the valley.

Square of Tiberius. To the east of the Square of Augustus stood a richly ornamented temple with Corinthian columns. The theatre lies in the western part of the city. Outside the city, on rising ground to the east, is the temple of Men Askainos, an important divinity in that part of Asia Minor.

The synagogue of Pisidian Antioch where Paul preached is not identified, but there were large Jewish colonies in the cities of Phrygia, both in Pisidian Antioch and in Iconium, the next city to which the two missionaries came.

Iconium lies nearly ninety miles east-south-east of Pisidian Antioch. The city and its name survive in modern Konya, the capital of the Turkish province of the same name. Then as now it

was an important junction: the main east–west road from Syria to Ephesus passed through it. The Emperor Claudius bestowed his own name on it as an honorary prefix: Claudiconium.

Lystra, to which Paul and Barnabas moved from Iconium, was about eighteen miles south of that city. It was identified in 1885 with the mound of Zostera (near the town of Hatunsaray), when J.R.S. Sterrett found a Latin inscription there containing the name of Lystra. Like Pisidian Antioch, Lystra was made a Roman colony by Augustus.

In passing from Iconium to Lystra Paul and Barnabas crossed the regional frontier from Phrygia into Lycaonia. (A region was a subdivision of a province.) Over 400 years previously the Greek historian Xenophon referred to Iconium as 'the last city of Phrygia'. If Paul and Barnabas had well-tuned ears, they would realise soon after leaving Iconium that the indigenous population spoke a language which they had not heard before – 'the speech of Lycaonia' mentioned in Acts 14:11. When the people of Lystra planned to pay them divine honours, the missionaries'

ignorance of this language meant that they did not grasp what was afoot until preparations for sacrificing to them were well advanced. Barnabas was identified with Zeus, the ruler of the gods, and Paul with Hermes, their messenger. There is evidence that these two divinities were worshipped conjointly in Lycaonia. In 1910 Sir William Calder discovered an inscription at Sedasa, south of Lystra, recording the dedication to Zeus of a statue of Hermes by men with Lycaonian names; sixteen years later he and W.H.Buckler discovered a stone altar near Lystra dedicated to the 'Hearer of Prayer' (presumably Zeus) and Hermes.

When Barnabas and Paul refused to accept worship from the people of Lystra, the people of Lystra soon turned against them: lending a ready ear to enemies of the missionaries who followed them from Iconium, they attacked them. Paul in particular was stoned, knocked unconscious and left for dead by the roadside (Acts 14:19). When, several years later, he drew up a catalogue of the hardships he had endured as an apostle, he says (referring to this occasion), 'Once I was stoned' (2 Corinthians 11:25).

Left: The stadium at Perge (ancient Perga) is one of the best preserved from antiquity. It would have seated an audience of about 12,000.

Right: A bronze coin of Lystra minted in the time of the Emperor Augustus, c 6 BC. The coin depicts the founder of Colonia Lystra tracing the limits of the new city with a plough drawn by a bull and cow.

Nevertheless, he had reason to remember his visit to Lystra with gratitude: one of his converts there was Timothy, his future travelling companion and faithful helper.

Derbe has been identified as recently as 1957, when Michael Ballance found evidence pointing to Kerti Hüyük (a mound about fifteen miles north-north-east of the city of Karaman) as the site. The evidence took the form of an inscription discovered on the mound, dedicated by the council and people of Derbe in AD 157 in honour of the Emperor Antoninus Pius.

Derbe lay some sixty miles south-east of Lystra, so that the last words of Acts 14:20 should be translated, 'he set out with Barnabas for Derbe.' (They should not be translated in such a way as to suggest that Paul, after being knocked about so badly the day before, walked the sixty miles to Derbe in one day.)

It has been suggested that Paul and Barnabas went no farther than Derbe because there they reached the

frontier of the province of Galatia. Across the frontier lay the territory of Antiochus, king of Commagene (AD 38–72), an ally of the Romans. Indeed, at times Derbe seems to have been governed by Antiochus; it was he who, in honour of the Emperor Claudius, named it Claudioderbe.

Above: The remains of the ancient stadium at Perga.

Macedonia

Macedonia is a large territory in the Balkan Peninsula, by far the greatest part of which now forms the northern province of Greece, while other parts lie in Yugoslavia and Bulgaria. In antiquity it was a powerful kingdom. The Greek city-states of the classical period (fifth and fourth centuries BC) did not consider the Macedonians to be proper Greeks, although the Macedonian kings were keen patrons of Greek culture. One of the greatest of these kings, Philip II (356–336 BC), conquered the Greek city-states and founded a Graeco-Macedonian empire. Scarcely had he done so when he was assassinated, but his twenty-year-old son Alexander took up his father's heritage and in 334 BC led a united Graeco-Macedonian army into Asia. In a few years he had overthrown the Persian Empire. When he died in 323

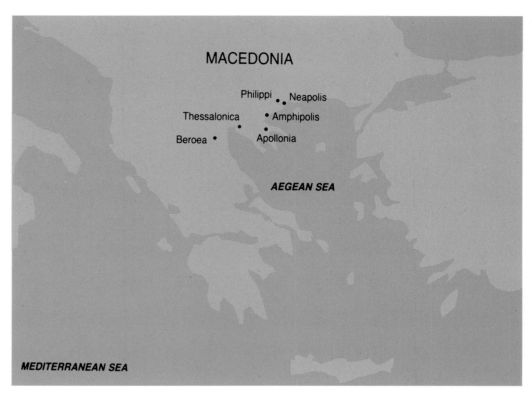

MACEDONIA

Philippi · Neapolis
Thessalonica · · Amphipolis
Beroea · Apollonia

AEGEAN SEA

MEDITERRANEAN SEA

Below: Kavalla, Greece (ancient Neapolis); it was here that Paul first set foot in Europe before making his way along the Egnatian Way to Philippi and Thessalonica.

BC his vast dominion did not long survive him as a united empire. Macedonia soon became a separate kingdom once more. From 221 BC relations between Macedonia and Rome were hostile, and after three wars Macedonia became a Roman province in 146 BC.

Christianity reached Macedonia not more than

'We travelled to Philippi, a Roman colony ... ' (Acts 16:12)

Right: The Roman market-place, or *agora*, at Philippi, built after the victory of Octavius at Philippi in 42 BC.

twenty years after the death of Christ. Acts 16:9 tells of Paul's night-vision at Troas in which a man of Macedonia appeared to him, saying, 'Come over into Macedonia and help us.' Paul shared his experience with his three companions, Silas, Timothy and Luke – and they agreed with him that this was a call from God. They took ship from Troas, therefore, and in two days they landed at Neapolis, the modern Kavalla.

Neapolis was the eastern terminus of the Egnatian Way, the east–west Roman military road which ran across the Balkan Peninsula, from the Aegean Sea to the Adriatic. It was the most direct route between Rome and the east. A well-preserved Roman aqueduct, with three tiers of arches, is still to be seen at Neapolis; it carried water to the acropolis which defended the old city.

Apart from Neapolis, Luke mentions five Macedonian cities which Paul and his companions visited on this occasion: Philippi, Amphipolis, Apollonia, Thessalonica and Beroea. The first four of these stood on the Egnatian Way.

Philippi lay about thirteen miles inland from Neapolis, which served as its port. Philippi bore the name of its founder, Philip of Macedonia: he established it in 356 BC on the site of an earlier settlement. Luke describes it in Acts 16:12 as a 'city of the first district of Macedonia' (the true reading is preserved only by a small minority of witnesses to the text). The 'first district' means the first of four districts into which the Romans divided Macedonia in 167 BC. Those familiar with Shakespeare's *Julius Caesar* remember how it was at Philippi that Caesar's assassins and their followers

clashed in battle with his lieutenant, Antony, and his adopted son, Octavian (later the Emperor Augustus). After the battle the victors, Antony and Octavian, re-constituted Philippi as a Roman colony and settled many of their veteran soldiers there (47 BC). As a Roman colony, Philippi had a constitution modelled on that of the city of Rome: it was governed by two annually appointed chief magistrates (called praetors), whose police attendants were called lictors. The magistrates and police figure in the story of Acts 16:19-39.

There was evidently no Jewish community of any size in Philippi. In most cities which they visited, Paul and his companions made for the local synagogue, but there was none in Philippi: instead they found an informal place of prayer outside the city on the west, by the river Gangites. Between the city and the river stand the

archaeologists between 1914 and 1938; more recently the work has been continued by the Greek archaeological service. The city stood both north and south of the Egnatian Way. The acropolis, over 1,000 feet high, on a spur of Mount Orbelos, overlooked the city from the north. At the foot of the hill are the remains of the large theatre, dating from the time of Philip II. On the south side of the Egnatian Way was the forum, some 300 by 100 feet. The forum buildings which can be seen today belong mostly to the age of Marcus Aurelius (AD 161–180), but they replaced others of an earlier period. It would have been in the forum that Paul and Silas were dragged before the praetors. In the centre of the north side of the forum was a speaker's platform; at the north-west and north-east corners stood two large temples. On the west side were grain-shops, on the east side a library and reading room; on the south side was a colonnade, with a Roman agora to the south of

Above: The cobbled Egnatian Way, the famous Roman road along which the Apostle Paul travelled. This stretch is near Kavalla, the ancient port of Neapolis.

Left: A view of the ancient forum at Philippi, looking towards Mount Pangaion.

remains of an arch, crossing the Egnatian way, which may have been built to commemorate the city's receiving the status of a colony. The place of prayer probably lay to the west of this arch. Here a group of women met every Sabbath day, and it was they who formed the nucleus of the church in Philippi. Their leader was Lydia, who traded in the purple dye for which

her native city, Thyatira in Asia Minor, was renowned. A Latin inscription in Philippi mentions dealers in purple there. Two other women in the Philippian church, Euodia and Syntyche, receive honourable mention from Paul because of their co-operation with him in his ministry of the gospel (Philippians 4:2,3).

The site of ancient Philippi was excavated by French

'They came to Thessalonica, where there was a Jewish synagogue ... ' (Acts 17:1)

Right: The Arch of Galerius, built to straddle the Egnatian Way as it entered ancient Thessalonica from the east.

Above: Remains of the ancient forum at Thessalonica, modern Salonika.

it, while farther south still were a palaestra or gymnasium and Roman baths. There are also remains of Christian basilicas, but they belong to the Byzantine period; they present features similar to those of St. Sophia in Istanbul.

Thessalonica lies about 90 miles west of Philippi. Paul and his friends did not cover that whole journey in one day. Amphipolis and Apollonia are mentioned by name in Acts 17:1 because they were places where the missionaries stayed at least overnight on the Egnatian Way from Philippi to Thessalonica.

Thessalonica was founded about 315 BC by the Macedonian king Cassander, who named it after his wife, a half-sister of Alexander the Great. When Macedonia became a Roman province, Thessalonica was the governor's headquarters, while it retained its municipal status as a free city, with its own magistrates, called 'politarchs' in Acts 17:6. This designation was peculiar to the magistrates of Macedonian cities; it appears on a number of inscriptions from the Roman period. The Egnatian Way ran through the city from east to west; part of the thoroughfare which follows its line, bears the same name today.

Since it is still a large and populous city, Thessalonica does not lend itself so well to archaeological excavation. Some of the monuments which do survive from Roman times, like the Arch of Galerius which straddled the Egnatian Way near the east gate of the ancient city, and the neighbouring Rotunda (later St. George's Church), belong to a much later date than Paul's lifetime – around AD 300. Until 1876 another arch, called the Vardar Gate, stood at the west end of the city: it bore an inscription (now in the British Museum) which mentioned the politarchs of Thessalonica.

Unlike Philippi, Thessalonica had a Jewish community with its synagogue, where Paul preached on the first three Sabbath days after his arrival in the city. Here, among the fringe of God-fearing Gentiles who attended the services, Paul found the

Above: Remains of the ancient city of Assos.

Above: A grotesque mask from an ancient Greek theatre.

nucleus of his church, but the majority of his converts were pagans who, as he said, 'turned to God from idols, to serve a living and true God' (1 Thessalonians 1:9).

Paul had to leave Thessalonica because he and his companions were accused before the magistrates of disseminating subversive propaganda. He had perhaps intended to travel farther west along the Egnatian Way, but he was obliged to turn south for some fifty miles until he reached the city of Beroea (now pronounced Verria). Here he was given a more open-minded reception by the synagogue authorities than he had found in Thessalonica. We have few details about his converts in Beroea, except that they included several Greek women of high standing (Acts 17:12), and that one of his male converts was Sopater, who a few years later was one of a party accompanying him on his last journey to Jerusalem (Acts 20:4). If (as is probable) he is identical with the Sosipater of Romans 16:21, he was evidently a Jew by birth, since Paul calls him 'my kinsman'.

Paul's first visit to Macedonia was punctuated by expulsions from one city after another. No wonder that when, a few weeks later, he arrived in Corinth, he could speak of coming 'in weakness and in much fear and trembling' (1 Corinthians 2:3). He possibly felt that his missionary work in Macedonia had been a failure. In fact it was an illustrious success. The Christianity which he planted in the cities of that province remains firmly rooted in the present day.

Athens

Athens has a continuous history of occupation as a Greek city from Mycenean times (before 1100 BC) to the present day. There was a short period during the Persian invasion under Xerxes in 480 BC when the Athenians had to leave their city and seek refuge on board their ships, but the invaders were soon defeated and the Athenians returned and rebuilt their ruined city. It remained a Greek city throughout the long centuries of Turkish rule. The Apostle Paul's brief visit to Athens, on his way from Macedonia to Corinth, is mentioned briefly by him in 1 Thessalonians 3:1 and is described at greater length by Luke in Acts 17:15-34.

Today it is the populous capital of Greece, but the heart of the city area is sufficiently cleared for the great monuments of its classical past to be conspicuously visible. Parts of a Mycenean defensive wall can be seen on the Acropolis, but most of the monuments date from the fifth century BC and later. Many of those that the visitor sees today were seen in a much better condition by Paul when he came to Athens in AD 50. Of all the buildings that crown the Acropolis the greatest is the Parthenon, the temple of Athene, the city's patron goddess. It was founded in 447 BC and even today is one of the most visually satisfying buildings to be seen anywhere in the world. In it stood the statue of Athene, the noblest work of the sculptor Pheidias. Some idea of the detail of the Parthenon can be appreciated in the sculptures from its pediment now in the British Museum, among the so-called Elgin Marbles. During the Christian era the Parthenon was used successively as a

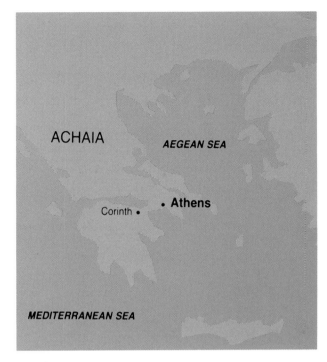

ACHAIA AEGEAN SEA

Corinth • • Athens

MEDITERRANEAN SEA

church, a mosque and an arsenal; this last use was nearly its total undoing when it was hit by a Venetian shell in 1687.

North of the Parthenon stands the temple of

Erechtheus, with its six sculptured maidens or Caryatids fulfilling the function of columns for its southern portico; west of it stands the temple of Wingless Victory. The temple of Wingless Victory is built against the southern wing of the great gateway or Propylaea through which the Panathenaic procession made its way on to the Acropolis once every four years to present a new robe for the primitive wooden image of Athene housed in the temple of Erechtheus. The procession came along the Panathenaic Way from the north-west, through the Sacred Gate in the city wall.

At the foot of the Acropolis, built into its southern slope, is the Theatre of Dionysus, where the great dramas of classical Athens were staged. North-west of the Acropolis lies the Agora, the great Athenian marketplace, adorned with public buildings and colonnades. One of the latter, the Stoa of Attalus, has been restored and serves today as the Agora Museum. It was in the Agora that Paul entered into daily debate during his

Above: A distant view of the Parthenon, seen from a point overlooking the ancient harbour.

Right: This head-on view of the Parthenon emphasizes its finely dimensioned structure.

'Paul stood up in the meeting of the Areopagus ... '
(Acts 17:22)

Left: The restored Stoa of Attalus, seen from the Acropolis. Recent research suggests that it may have been here that Paul addressed the Court (or meeting) of the Areopagus.

Above: Inside the splendidly restored Stoa of Attalus, Athens.

stay in Athens 'with those who chanced to be there', including philosophers of the Epicurean and Stoic schools, both of which had their headquarters in Athens (Acts 17:17, 18).

Paul took everything in, but in his day the temples, altars and images were no mere antiquities or works of art, but installations of an active worship, false worship at that. 'His spirit was provoked within him as he saw that the city was full of idols' (Acts 17:16). One altar, however, attracted his special attention because of its unusual dedication: 'To an unknown god'. Other visitors to Athens about this time mention as a mark of the city's exceptional religiosity the 'anonymous altars' – altars to unknown gods – which it contained.

Why the altar spotted by Paul bore this particular inscription we cannot know. Perhaps, as has happened elsewhere, it was an old altar repaired by people who had no means of discovering the divinity to which it was originally dedicated, so they dedicated it 'to an unknown god'. But Paul saw how he could make use of this strange wording.

There was a venerable court in Athens which had jurisdiction in matters of religion and morals. Since Paul, with his talk of Jesus and the resurrection, seemed to be recommending a new religion, he was brought before it. It was called the Court of the Areopagus, because it met originally on the Areopagus, the hill of the war-god Ares, which rises on the west side of the Acropolis. By the first century AD, however, except on specially solemn occasions, the court is believed to have met in the Royal Colonnade

Right: Statue of Athene, from the museum at Antalya.

Right: Relief of an ancient Greek chariot from Athens.

in the Agora, and it may have been there that it examined Paul. The statement that he was brought 'to the Areopagus' (Acts 17:19) may simply mean that he was brought before the court, and when he is described as 'standing in the middle of the Areopagus' (Acts 17:22) this probably means that he stood in the midst of the court, with its members sitting around him, rather than that he 'stood in the midst of Mars hill', as the Authorised Version says. (How does one stand in the middle of a hill?)

No matter: when he was invited to expound his teaching, Paul referred to the Athenians as 'very religious' and recalled the altar inscription which had made such an impression on him. The 'unknown God' mentioned in the inscription was the very God whom he had come to make known, he said – the God who created all things and who, far from requiring anything from men and women, provided them with all that they needed. He supported his claims with quotations from Greek poets – 'In him we live and move and have our being' and 'we are indeed his offspring' (Acts 17:28). He then urged his hearers to have worthy thoughts of this God, who would call them to give an account one day to the man whom he had raised from the dead. Any who responded to Paul's preaching might well be said, like the pagans of Thessalonica, to have 'turned to God from idols, to serve a living and true God, and to wait for his Son from heaven, whom he raised from the dead, Jesus, who delivers us from the wrath to come' (1 Thessalonians 1:9, 10).

To most of Paul's hearers, this talk of a man being raised from the dead was absurd. He probably felt that he had achieved very little in Athens. A few converts are mentioned, but we find no reference to a church in Athens in Paul's day. Yet Athens was in due course to embrace wholeheartedly the message which he brought. The text of his address to the Areopagus is engraved on a bronze tablet at the foot of the ascent to the hill. A thoroughfare west of the hill is called 'Street of the Apostle Paul', and running off it towards the east, on the south side of the Acropolis, is the 'Street of Dionysius the Areopagite' (Paul's principal Athenian convert). Paul would be surprised, but no doubt gratified, could he know that his visit and preaching have been so well remembered.

Corinth

Corinth was an ancient city of Greece; its name, at least, goes back to pre-Greek times. It was situated on the Isthmus of Corinth (which was called after it) – the narrow neck of land which joins Central Greece to the Peloponnese, the peninsula which forms the southern part of mainland Greece. By its position it dominated the north–south land route, and it was equipped with two harbours. The western harbour, Lechaeon, on the Gulf of Corinth, communicated with the central and western Mediterranean; the eastern harbour, Cenchreae (mentioned in Acts 18:18 and Romans 16:1), communicated with the Aegean Sea and through it with the Black Sea and the eastern Mediterranean.

The ancient city was built on the north side of the hill called Acrocorinthus, which rises to a height of 1,900 feet and served it as a citadel. The citadel had an inexhaustible water supply in the upper spring of Peirene; a lower spring of the same name provided water for the city itself. Modern Corinth does not stand on the site of Old Corinth, but some three miles to the north; the site of Old Corinth therefore is completely accessible to archaeological exploration.

In classical Greek times Corinth attained great commercial prosperity; its name also became proverbial for licentiousness. It was a centre of the worship of Aphrodite, the goddess of love, whose temple stood on the summit of the Acrocorinthus. At the foot of the hill stood the temple of Melicertes, the patron of seafarers. The Isthmian Games, over which Corinth presided, and in which all Greek cities participated, were held every two years. At

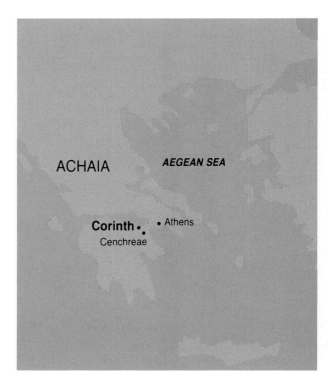

these games the sea-god Poseidon was specially honoured. Corinth paid respect, as Paul put it, to 'many "gods" and many "lords" ' (1 Corinthians 8:5).

Greek Corinth was utterly

Right: Cenchreae, the port of ancient Corinth. The Acropolis of Corinth can be seen in the distance (far right). Paul embarked at Cenchreae when he travelled on from Corinth to Ephesus.

Above: The Acrocorinth, with the Lechaion Road in the foreground. This road led from the centre of the ancient city to its western port on the Gulf of Corinth.

Right: The Fountain of Peirene, Corinth, a natural spring of great antiquity which has been so heavily remodelled that it now appears to be an artificial fountain. The water is stored in four long reservoirs fed by a transverse supply tunel.

destroyed by a Roman army in 146 BC; this was its punishment for the leading part which it had played in a revolt against Rome. The only building of importance surviving from the period before that destruction is the Doric temple of Apollo, erected in the sixth century BC; seven great monolithic columns of this building still dominate the site. The city lay derelict for a century; then, in 44 BC, it was refounded as a Roman colony by Julius Caesar. Roman Corinth quickly regained the prosperity which Greek Corinth had enjoyed. The main roads and the two harbours were still at its disposal; in addition, a railroad of wooden logs, three and a half miles in length, was laid from west to east across the Isthmus so that ships might be dragged on it from the one harbour to the other. This railroad was called the *diolkos*.

Since Corinth was a Roman colony, all its citizens were Romans. It had many other residents, both Greeks and

'Paul stayed on in Corinth for some time ... '
Acts 18:18)

Jews, who were not citizens. One of Paul's earliest converts in Corinth, Gaius (1 Corinthians 1:14; Romans 16:23), was probably a Roman citizen; it is commonly believed that he is identical with the Titius Justus of Acts 18:7, and if so, then he bore an authentic threefold Roman name: Gaius Titius Justus.

When Paul first came to Corinth (in the autumn of AD 50), he visited the synagogue and was permitted, for a few weeks, to preach the gospel there, expounding the Sabbath lessons from the Old Testament in such a way as to show that they pointed forward to Jesus. The museum of Old Corinth contains part of a stone lintel with a Greek inscription which, when entire, read 'Synagogue of the Hebrews'. If it did not stand over the doorway of the very synagogue where Paul preached (which is not

impossible), it belonged to a building which replaced the synagogue of Paul's day.

Another inscription, found in Corinth by American archaeologists in 1929, was engraved on a marble slab; it informs us in Latin that 'Erastus, in commemoration of his aedileship (curatorship of public buildings), laid this pavement at his own expense'. The inscription seems to belong to the first century AD and refers, in all

probability, to that Erastus who is mentioned in Romans 16:23 as 'city treasurer' of Corinth. If this is so, then we should gather that Erastus performed his duties as aedile so well that he was promoted to a higher and more responsible of office.

When Paul in 1 Corinthians 10:25 refers to people in Corinth buying meat in the 'meat market', he uses the Greek word *makellon*. This word has been found in

Left: This inscription, found on a pavement at Corinth, includes the name of Erastus, the city treasurer, and probably the official mentioned in Romans 16:23.

Below: Remains of the Doric Temple of Apollo, Corinth, the only major building to survive the Roman rebuilding of the city.

Right: A Roman relief of a husband and wife.

Right: A larger than life-size marble statue of a barbarian slave from Corinth; it is one of a pair which helped support the roof of a two-storey stoa in the Roman agora.

another Corinthian inscription which indicates that the meat market was situated somewhere along the paved Lechaeon Road. Many shops and colonnades have been uncovered by archaeologists around the fine square Roman agora (market-place). In the centre of the agora is an impressive stone platform which figures in the New Testament narrative. This is the 'tribunal' from which Gallio pronounced judgment when Paul was accused before him of propagating an illegal religion (Acts 18:12-17). Corinth, in addition to being a Roman colony, was the seat of administration of the Roman province of Achaia. When Gallio was sent from Rome to be proconsul of Achaia in AD 51, it was in Corinth that he took up residence. He refused to take up the case against Paul, because he concluded that the dispute was over rival interpretations of the Jewish law. But his judgement, though negative, was in effect a favourable one so far as Paul was concerned; it confirmed his liberty to carry on with his apostolic work. An adverse judgement would have been a great handicap to him, for Gallio was an important and influential person, whose verdict would be followed as a precedent by many Roman magistrates throughout the empire.

A Turbulent Church

Paul arrived at Corinth in a mood of dejection and apprehension. He had practically been driven out of Macedonia, and his reception in Athens had been lukewarm. Corinth had probably not figured on his original itinerary, and the reputation of the city was such that he could scarcely expect the gospel to make much of an impact there. He was greatly in need of the heavenly encouragement which came to him in a night vision shortly after his arrival in Corinth. But he stayed in Corinth for eighteen months (Acts 18:9,10), and when he moved on at the end of that period, he left behind him a large and gifted, if volatile, church. It is plain from his two letters to the Corinthians that the church which he planted there caused him many a headache: it was turbulent and unruly, but it was undoubtedly alive, and remains so to this day.

Ephesus

Above: Coin of the Emperor Maximus, AD 235-238, depicting the Temple of Artemis (Diana) at Ephesus.

Right: The view from the top tiers of the great theatre at Ephesus, showing the long, straight Arcadian Way leading in the distance to the ancient harbour, long since silted over.

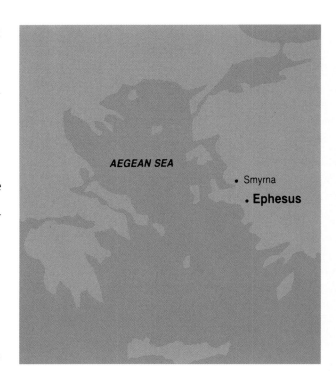

AEGEAN SEA

• Smyrna

• **Ephesus**

Ephesus stood at the mouth of the river Caÿster, which flows into the Aegean Sea. In the days before the Greeks (more precisely, the Ionians) colonised that part of western Asia Minor, there was a settlement of Carians on the site. These Carians worshipped the great mother-goddess of Asia Minor and probably called her Artemis – the name is non-Greek. When the Ionian colonists arrived, they intermarried with the Carians and joined in the worship of their goddess. Artemis first appears in art and literature as the guardian of wild-life. Her temple at Ephesus housed her image, which was believed to have 'fallen from the sky' (Acts 19:35). An earlier temple than that which stood there in New Testament times was burned down in 356 BC – on the very night, people said, when Alexander the Great was born. The young man who set fire to it said that he had done so in order that his name might go down in history. He achieved his aim, for if we know nothing else about him, we know his name – it was Herostratus.

The magnificent temple which replaced the one burnt by Herostratus was one of the seven wonders of the ancient world. It covered an area four times as extensive as the Parthenon in Athens; it was supported by 127 columns, each of them sixty feet high, and it was adorned by some of the greatest sculptors of the age. But it disappeared completely; for centuries no one knew where it had stood, until its site was identified beyond all doubt on the last day of 1869 by J. T. Wood. Its foundations were then discovered in a marsh at the foot of the hill of Ayasoluk, near the town known today as Selçuk. On the hill of Ayasoluk stand the remains of a later shrine – the basilica of St. John the Divine, erected by the Emperor Justinian (AD 527–565). Its high altar covers the traditional tomb of John. The very name Ayasoluk preserves the apostle's memory: it is a

'Great is Artemis of the Ephesians.'
(Acts 19:28)

Opposite: The splendidly restored Library of Celsus in Ephesus gives some idea of the wonder of the city in ancient times.

Right: The view down the Arcadian Way, the magnificent paved road leading from the centre of Ephesus to the ancient harbour.

Right: A monumental gateway near the Library of Celsus, Ephesus.

corruption of the Greek phrase meaning the 'holy divine'.

Roman Ephesus, the city that Paul knew, stood about one and a half miles south or south-west of the temple of Artemis. Its site is an archaeologist's paradise, for it is unencumbered by any modern settlement. The whole area has for many years been excavated systematically by Austrian archaeologists, and as successive streets and buildings are uncovered and restored, they make a magnificent impression.

In New Testament times Ephesus was a seaport; the harbour had to be dredged continuously to clear it of the silt washed down by the river Caÿster. As the city decayed, the harbour was neglected, and today Ephesus stands seven miles inland. As one looks out from the topmost tiers of the theatre it is possible to discern the

Above: It was on this marshy site that the renowned Temple of Artemis (or Diana) stood in Paul's day. One column has been reconstructed to give some concept of the size of the great edifice. Behind can be seen the citadel, enclosing the site of the Basilica of St. John.

outline of the ancient harbour, almost as in aerial photography; it is now a marshy waste at the end of the paved street called the Arcadian Way. To the right of the Arcadian Way, as one looks down from the theatre, stand the twin churches of St. Mary, in which the Council of Ephesus was held in AD 431. The theatre itself, a vast open-air auditorium built into the western slope of Mount Pion, could seat 24,000 people. The civic assembly regularly met in the theatre on appointed dates. The theatre was also the venue for the very irregular assembly which Luke describes in Acts 19:29-41, when the populace staged a two-hour demonstration in honour of 'Great Artemis of the Ephesians' and in opposition to Paul and his associates.

There is no evidence that Paul spoke disparagingly in public about the great goddess: in fact, the town clerk of Ephesus, in the speech which he made to quieten the demonstrators in the theatre, absolved him and his associates of any such

Left: A statue of Artemis, the many-breasted goddess, from Ephesus.

offence. But every one knew that he did not believe in her, and when he made converts among the pagans of Ephesus, they abandoned her worship. This naturally caused concern to those whose livelihood depended on her worship, like the guild of silversmiths, who manufactured prodigious souvenirs and amulets, and miniature replicas of the goddess in her shrine. Silver reproductions of her image and terracotta models of her temple have been found. An inscription of AD 104, half a century after Paul's visit, tells how a Roman official presented a silver image of Artemis, together with other statues, to be set up in the theatre during a meeting of the civic assembly.

Demetrius, president of the guild of silversmiths, had reason to be concerned at the threat to his trade. But his concern was not purely economic: he is described in terms which suggest that he was one of the twelve members of the 'vestry' of the temple of Artemis. And what he feared came to pass – not immediately, but in the course of a few centuries: the advance of the gospel inevitably meant the diminishing of the worship of Artemis, until at last she was 'deposed from her magnificence' (Acts 19:27). Then, centuries later, people of yet another faith took possession of the country, and the churches of St. Mary and St. John fell into ruins in their turn. But the record of Paul's ministry in Ephesus, and the two letters to the Ephesians in the New Testament – one by Paul, the other from the risen Lord through his servant John (Revelation 2:1-7) – remain as a powerful proclamation of the Christian gospel.

We do not know where

Above: The Fountain of Trajan, Ephesus. A huge statue of the Emperor originally stood in the middle section of the building.

'Paul has convinced ... large numbers of people here in Ephesus ... ' (Acts 19:26)

Right: Statue of the god of the river Maeander beside the remains of one of the huge pools at Baths of Faustina, Miletus, where Paul said farewell to the elders of the church of Ephesus (Acts 20:17).

Paul lived in Ephesus. The Jewish synagogue in which he preached during the first few weeks of his stay has not been located yet, nor is there any means of identifying the school of Tyrannus, where for two years he lectured around midday, when Tyrannus and his pupils were taking their siesta. We know that Paul was exposed to repeated dangers during his Ephesian ministry. On an eminence to the south of the former harbour stands a ruin which is called 'St. Paul's Prison'. It has no historical title to be so called, but the tradition that Paul was imprisoned for a period while he was in Ephesus may be well founded.

Near the Magnesian Gate, south-east of Mount Pion, an early Christian shrine has been identified in a cave, with graffiti invoking Paul. But in Christian tradition the great name associated with Ephesus is that of John. Not only so, but in view of the statement in John 19:27 that the beloved disciple took the mother of Jesus to his own home after the crucifixion, it came to be believed that when he migrated to Ephesus she accompanied him. One testimony to this belief is presented by the twin churches of St. Mary already mentioned; another, overlooking the site of Ephesus, is a building venerated since 1891 as the house of the Virgin Mary; it has received no official recognition, but has twice in recent years been honoured by a papal visit.

Right: Ancient sculpture of a lion, from the Baths of Faustina, Miletus.

From Opposition to Opportunity

Towards the end of his long missionary stay in Ephesus, Paul wrote to his friends in Corinth, promising to pay them a visit soon, but, he added, 'I will stay in Ephesus until Pentecost, for a wide door for effective work has opened to me, and there are many adversaries' (1 Corinthians 16:8,9). He was writing probably about Easter (in AD 55), and he had been in Ephesus for two and a half years. Great opportunities and great opposition were to Paul familiar experiences in his apostolic work, and each was usually accompanied by the other. By this stage in his career Paul had learned how to turn opposition into opportunity, and so thoroughly did he prosecute his ministry in Ephesus that Christianity persisted in that part of Asia Minor for centuries after the Turkish conquest, and disappeared only with the wholesale exchange of Greek and Turkish populations which followed the Graeco-Turkish war of 1923.

Caesarea

Caesarea Maritima – Caesarea-on-Sea, as we might say – was built by Herod the Great between 22 and 9 BC to serve as an adequate seaport on the Mediterranean coast of Judea. There was an earlier settlement there, with a fortification called Straton's Tower, called after a Sidonian ruler who flourished about 330 BC. We know that a harbour of sorts had been constructed there by 259 BC, for it is mentioned in one of the Zenon papyri, a collection of documents from an Egyptian finance officer (at that time Palestine belonged to the kingdom of the Egyptian Ptolemies).

Excavations at Caesarea completed since 1959 have revealed something of the magnificent scale of Herod's buildings, but most impressive of all was the great artificial harbour, enclosed by two massive stone breakwaters. These were examined in 1960 by the

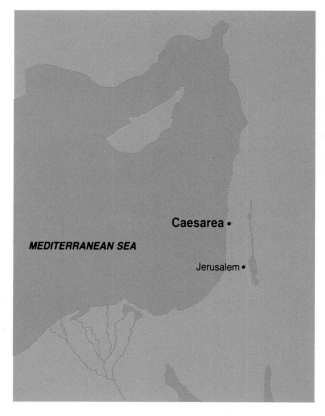

Link Mission for Underwater Exploration, and it was established that they enclosed a semicircular area of about three and a half acres. Josephus describes the huge blocks of stone which were let down into twenty fathoms of water to serve as foundations for the breakwaters. The entry to the harbour was from the north-west. The harbour installations were on a scale appropriate to such an engineering masterpiece. An earthquake in AD 130 caused considerable damage to the structures.

Two parallel aqueducts conveyed water to Caesarea – one of Herod's period, bringing water from springs on the southern slope of Carmel, and a later one bringing a further supply from the Crocodile River, about six miles north of Caesarea.

Herod called the city Caesarea, after his patron Caesar Augustus. A fine temple in the emperor's house, probably dedicated to 'Rome and Augustus', was erected on an artificial mound of stone, fifty feet high, facing the harbour. The

Below: View along the top of the Roman aqueduct, built to convey water to the ancient port of Caesarea Maritima.

51

'King Agrippa and Bernice arrived at Caesarea to pay their respects to Festus ... ' (Acts 25:13)

Opposite: The well-preserved Roman aqueduct at Caesarea Maritima.

Right: A view of the harbour at Caesarea from the Roman theatre.

Right: Part of the warehouse complex of the Roman harbour at Caesarea.

Below: Coin of the Procurator Pontius Pilate.

royal palace also stood on this mound. The vaulted chambers which supported the mound are still to be seen today.

In the southern part of the city Herod built a theatre facing the sea. This was excavated about 1960 by Italian archaeologists. Its acoustic properties can readily be tested; they bear witness to the skill with which it was constructed. One stone found there contains part of a Latin inscription in which Pontius Pilate, 'prefect of Judea' (AD 26–36), is said to have dedicated a public building in honour of the Emperor Tiberius (AD 14–37). During a later reconstruction of the theatre the stone was built into the steps; the reconstructors did not realise how important the inscription would be for future archaeologists.

Further east from the theatre, Herod built a hippodrome, while to the north of the city there was an

amphitheatre, used for athletic sports and for gladiatorial and wild beast shows.

The history of Caesarea continues into Byzantine and Crusader times. Among Byzantine buildings are successive synagogues of the fourth and fifth century (probably on the site where the Herodian synagogue stood) and a Christian building (apparently not a church) which contained a statue of the good shepherd and a mosaic showing a quotation from Romans 13:3.

Caesarea in New Testament times was a predominantly Gentile city, though it had a considerable Jewish population. When Judea became a Roman province in AD 6 and was administered by a succession of governors appointed by the emperor, the governors took up residence in Caesarea. When public order required their presence in Jerusalem, as at the great pilgrimage festivals, they moved there; but normally they felt more at home in Caesarea. There the royal palace that Herod had built for himself served as their residence. In Acts 23:35 it is called 'Herod's praetorium' (praetorium being a technical term for the commander-in-chief's headquarters). The governors of Judea who figure in the New Testament – Pilate, Felix, Festus – all resided here. As the governors were supreme commanders of the Roman military forces in the province, detachments of Roman troops were regularly stationed in Caesarea.

When Paul paid a brief visit to Jerusalem in the third year after his conversion to make the acquaintance of two leaders of the mother-church, Peter and James, his presence in the city became known to his enemies. His new friends therefore judged that it would be best for his safety – and no doubt for theirs – if he left Jerusalem as soon as

possible, so some of them escorted him to Caesarea and put him on board a ship bound for his native Tarsus. As they watched its sails disappear over the horizon, they probably breathed a sigh of relief. 'Then the church had peace,' writes Luke (Acts 9:31).

Paul was not the only apostle to visit Caesarea; Peter went there on at least one occasion, when he was sent to preach the gospel to the Roman centurion Cornelius, a non-commissioned officer of the Augustan cohort (Acts 10:1-8).

It was in Caesarea that Herod Agrippa the elder (grandson of the city's founder) was making a public oration at a festival in honour of the Emperor Claudius when he was suddenly attacked by severe internal pains which ended

only with his death five days later (AD 44). The incident is recorded by Luke (Acts 12:21-23) and, in rather greater detail, by Josephus.

When Paul completed his last voyage from Greece to Palestine, together with a number of companions from his Gentile mission-field (Luke among them), he arrived at Caesarea and there the party spent several days in the house of Philip the evangelist. Twenty years previously Philip, after his mission in Samaria and his fruitful meeting on the Gaza road with the royal treasurer from Ethiopia, travelled north along the Mediterranean coastal road, evangelising each place to which he came, until he arrived in Caesarea (Acts 8:4-40). There he appears to have settled down and raised a family; when Paul and his companions visited him they were impressed by Philip's four daughters, each one a prophetess. Many years later, when these daughters were old ladies, they lived at Hierapolis in Phrygia and were much sought after as informants about persons and events in the early church.

Paul and his friends then left Caesarea for Jerusalem, but in less than two weeks Paul was back in Caesarea, through no choice of his own. He was taken into protective custody by the Roman army in Jerusalem, to save him from being beaten to death by a hostile mob in the temple precincts, and when the commanding officer in the Antonia fortress discovered that he was a Roman citizen, he decided to send him for safety to Caesarea. To Caesarea, then, he sent him under armed guard to Felix (Roman governor of Judea from AD 52-59). There Paul was kept in Herod's praetorium for two years, until Felix was replaced as governor by Festus. Then, fearing that Festus' inexperience might expose him to his enemies in Jerusalem all over again, Paul exercised his privilege as a Roman citizen and appealed to have his case transferred to the tribunal of the emperor in Rome. It was at Caesarea, on the eve of his being sent to Rome, that Paul had the opportunity of giving an account of his conversion and ministry before Herod Agrippa the younger (son of that Herod Agrippa who had met a sudden death in Caesarea fifteen years before).

Above: Some of the columns from the ancient harbour of Caesarea can be seen here, embedded in the harbour walls.

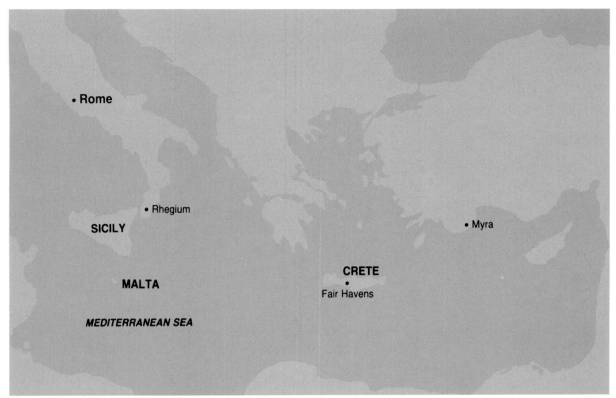

Right: St. Paul's Bay, Malta, the traditional site of the Apostle's shipwreck.

Right: A Roman ship leaving harbour, depicted on an ancient lamp.

During Paul's imprisonment in Caesarea (AD 57–59), tension between the Gentile and Jewish populations of the city increased to the point where outbreaks of violence took place between the two communities. The ineptitude with which this trouble was handled by the provincial administration and even by the authorities in Rome played its part in fostering the anti-Roman feeling among the Jews of Judea which came to a head in the revolt of AD 66.

Rome

Rome was in Paul's day the greatest city in the world, dominating the whole Mediterranean area, with all Europe west of the Rhine and south of the Danube, and all south-western Asia west of the Euphrates.

It is difficult for us, in this day of great super-powers, to realise how a single city could create for itself a power-base from which it could control a great part of the known world. Yet history knows of many such cities, and Rome is the best known of all.

Rome originated as a group of pastoral hill-settlements in the plain of Latium in Italy, on the left bank of the Tiber, about fifteen miles upstream from the mouth of the river. These settlements combined to form a city, which by stages dominated the plain of Latium, then the greater part of Italy, then Sicily and Sardinia, and so, after conquering the rival city of Carthage in modern Tunisia, to the mastery of the Mediterranean world.

As this empire extended, citizenship of Rome was not confined to freeborn natives of the capital: it was conferred, judiciously, on people in the provinces who had served Roman interests in some outstanding way, and once a man received Roman citizenship, all his descendants inherited the honour. Paul, a native of the province of Cilicia, was born a Roman citizen (Acts 22:28), which means that his father must have been one before him.

It was only after many years of apostolic activity in the eastern provinces of the

ITALY

• Rome

• Puteoli   Brindisi •

SICILY

Below: A general view looking south-east from the Capitoline Hill over the forum of ancient Rome. The great Colosseum, built after Paul's time, can be seen in the background.

'And so we came to Rome ... '
(Acts 28:14)

Right: The massive walls of the Colosseum, Rome, built to house spectacular games and contests for the Roman public.

Below: Part of the Imperial Forum, Rome.

Roman Empire that Paul at last had the opportunity of visiting the city of which he was a citizen by birth. He had set out for it more than once before, but had always been side-tracked. When he first came to Philippi and Thessalonica, he found himself on the Egnatian Way, which ran west to the Adriatic coast, from which there was a short sea-crossing to Brindisi in Italy, and from there the Appian Way led to Rome. Perhaps even then he had some idea of following this route, but he was prevented from doing so, and turned south instead of proceeding west. Nearly ten years later he achieved his ambition of seeing Rome, but in a way which he could not have

when Christianity was first brought to Rome. Priscilla and Aquila, who were among the Jews expelled from Rome by the Emperor Claudius in AD 49, met Paul in Corinth next year and became his firm and lifelong friends. Yet he never speaks of them as though they were converts of his, and the probability is that they were members of the primitive Christian community in Rome before they were forced to leave the city.

Having arrived in Rome, then, Paul spent the next two years there, 'in his own hired house', as the AV says – not an exact translation, perhaps, but one that spells out what is really meant by the RSV 'at his own expense'. Where he stayed in Rome we can only guess – possibly on the third floor of a tenement, where the rent would be cheaper. He was not free to come and go as he chose, because he was constantly handcuffed to a soldier. The soldier was relieved by a comrade every few hours, but there was no

Above: The Mamertine Prison, Rome, built some 2500 years ago, and probably where the Apostle was imprisoned.

foreseen. He came to Rome as a prisoner, under military guard, to stand his trial before the emperor, to whose jurisdiction he had appealed from the provincial court in Judea.

By the time Paul reached Rome (early in AD 60) there were many Christians there. Three years previously Paul had written a letter to the Christians in Rome (presented in our New Testament as the Letter to the Romans) to prepare them for his projected visit – which at that time he hoped to pay as a free agent. When at last he was being taken to the city along the final stages of the Appian Way, some Roman Christians walked out along the road for thirty or forty miles to greet him and escort him for the remainder of his journey. The sight of these friends brought Paul much encouragement.

It is impossible to be sure

Left: The Roman forum, viewed from the Palatine Hill. On the far left is the Capitol Hill; three remaining pillars of the Temple of Castor and Pollux can also be seen. Behind the Arch of Septimius Severus may be seen the entrance to the Mamertine Prison.

Above: The Appian Way, the main route followed by Paul on his journey to Rome.

Opposite: The Arch of Titus, built to commemorate the Emperor's victories in the East.

Right: Within the arch is a famous relief depicting Roman soldiers bearing Jewish trophies from Jerusalem.

such relief for Paul.

Visitors to Rome are shown the Mamertine prison, north-west of the Roman forum, as the place where both Paul and Peter spent their last days in the condemned cell. If there is any truth in this tradition, so far as Paul is concerned, it must refer to a later phase than the two years of Acts 28:30. That Paul was ultimately condemned to death and led out for execution by the third milestone along the Ostian Way is reasonably certain, although there is no record of this in the New Testament. The traditional site of his execution by the sword may be seen today in the monastic enclosure of Tre Fontane; the great basilica of St. Paul Outside the Walls covers the traditional site of his tomb. The present basilica, completed in 1854, replaces a magnificent fourth-century structure, which was accidentally burned down in 1823. In the first century the

'Boldly he preached the kingdom of God … '
(Acts 28:31)

Right: Part of the garden of the Abbey of Three Fountains, three miles outside Rome on the Ostian Way. By tradition, this is the site of Paul's execution, during Nero's persecution of Christians.

area was a public burial-ground; so, incidentally, was the area covered by St. Peter's in Vatican City, where the apostle Peter is (with good reason) believed to have been buried.

As today we view the monuments of imperial Rome, we have to remind ourselves that some of the most familiar of them were not there in the apostles' time. The Roman Forum was there, and the Sacred Way ran through it, but there was no Arch of Titus at the east end nor Arch of Septimus Severus at the west end. The best known of Roman monuments, the Colosseum, was begun ten or twelve years after Paul's death.

On the other hand, Paul saw much that cannot be seen today. He saw the city as it had been restored by the Emperor Augustus (27 BC – AD 14), who boasted that he had 'found a city of brick and left a city of marble'. Just over

four years after Paul's arrival, the great fire of Rome broke out (in July, AD 64) and destroyed a good part of the city. As is well known, the fire was followed by Nero's

victimisation of the Christians of Rome. Tradition assures us that Peter and Paul were the most distinguished victims of this persecution, but it certainly claimed as martyrs a

Right: St. Paul Outside the Walls, the great basilica built over the traditional site of the Apostle's burial.

Left: A simple inscription in one of the catacombs in Rome.

great number of ordinary Christians who have left behind no name.

As Paul first approached Rome by the Appian Way, he saw by the roadside some monuments which survive, if only in a ruined condition, to our own day – the tomb of Cecilia Metella, for example, and, nearer the city, the tomb of the Scipios. As he was led out of the city along the Ostian Way he would have seen the pyramid of Gaius Cestius (but the wall of Aurelian, into which it is now built, is 200 years later than Paul's time).

There was a large Jewish population in Rome in Paul's time; almost as many Jews lived in Rome as normally lived in Jerusalem. No synagogue of the period has yet been identified in Rome (a synagogue in Ostia, the port of ancient Rome, was excavated in 1963). But six Jewish catacombs or underground burial areas have been discovered around Rome, and from inscriptions in these we know the names of eleven Roman synagogues. The ordinary Romans of this period cremated their dead, but Jews (and, in due course, Christians) buried theirs, and so the bodies had to be

deposited at a deeper level. The soft tufa limestone of the district around Rome was rather easily tunnelled, and galleries were driven through it lined with recesses in which the dead were placed. None of the Christian catacombs of Rome goes back to New Testament times, but the earliest go back to the second century. One of the earliest is the Cemetery of Priscilla on the Via Salaria, but what connection it has with Paul's friend of that name is uncertain.

Left: Sculpted head of the Emperor Nero.

Babylon the Great

The book of the Revelation was written against the background of the persecution of Christians by the Roman Empire. Rome is prominent in the book, but not by name. She is referred to as 'Babylon the great', situated on seven hills, 'the great city which has dominion over the kings of the earth' (Revelation 14:8). In language similar to that used by Old Testament prophets to proclaim the downfall of oppressive powers in their days, the impending destruction of 'Babylon the great' is described. But what happened? The empire ultimately capitulated to the church, and Rome became a great Christian metropolis. John's Master taught that the best way to destroy an enemy is to turn him into a friend, and John might have been surprised, but not displeased, could he have foreseen that, 250 years after his day, the persecuting city would embrace the faith which once it tried to exterminate.

Index

Picture Acknowledgements

Jamie Simson: pp. 12, 13, 14, 31, 32, 44
Ancient Art & Architecture Collection: p. 7
Maurice S. Thompson (Bible Scene): pp. 6 (top), 8, 9, 10, 11, 13, 19, 20, 21, 22, 23, 24, 26 (top), 27, 33, 34, 35, 36, 38 (top), 39 (bottom), 41, 42, 43, 45 (bottom), 48 (top), 51, 52 (top), 54 (bottom) 55 (top and bottom left), 56, 58 (bottom), 59, 60 (top), 62, 63, front cover
Tiger Design Ltd: All remaining photographs

In the Steps of the Apostle Paul
by F.F. Bruce

Published in 1995 by Kregel Publications, a division of Kregel Inc., P. O. Box 2607, Grand Rapids, MI 49501. Kregel Publications provides trusted, biblical publications for Christian growth and service. Your comments and suggestions are valued.

This text originally appeared as part of *Places They Knew: Jesus and Paul* (1981) and is used here by kind permission of Scripture Union Publishing

Designed and created by
Three's Company
5 Dryden Street,
London WC2E 9NW

Library of Congress Cataloging-in-Publication Data
Bruce, F.F. (Frederick Fyvie), 1910-1990
  In the steps of the Apostle Paul/F.F. Bruce.
    p. cm.
    Includes index.
    1. Paul, the Apostle, Saint—Journeys—Mediterranean Region. 2. Mediterranean Region—Description and travel. I. Title.
BS2506.B746   1995
225.9'1—dc20   95-9694
                              CIP
ISBN 0-8254-2254-x (hardcover)
2 3 4 5 Printing/Year 99 98 97

Printed in Singapore